# About Skill Builders Spelling

## by Jennifer Thompson and Hollie Hendricks

**W**elcome to RBP Books' Skill Builders series. Like our Summer Bridge Activities collection, the Skill Builders series is designed to make learning both fun and rewarding.

This workbook is based on core curriculum and designed to reinforce classroom spelling skills and strategies for second graders. This workbook holds students' interest with the right mix of challenge, imagination, and instruction. The diverse assignments teach spelling while giving the students something fun to think about—from "barking lots" to the kitchen sink. As students complete the workbook, they will be well prepared to challenge themselves with more difficult words and vocabulary. A critical thinking section includes exercises to help develop higher-order thinking skills.

Learning is more effective when approached with an element of fun and enthusiasm—just as most children approach life. That's why the Skill Builders combine entertaining and academically sound exercises with eye-catching graphics and fun themes—to make reviewing basic skills at school or home fun and effective, for both you and your budding scholars.

# Table of Contents

Read the words in the word list. Listen to the short vowel sounds. Write the missing letters in the circles. The letters in the circles will give you the answer to this riddle. If you took a dog downtown, where would you leave it?

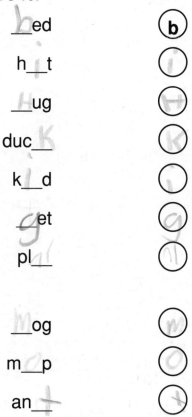

_bed        (**b**)

h_i_t        (i)

_H_ug        (H)

duc_K_        (K)

k_i_d        (i)

_g_et        (g)

pl_u_        (u)


_M_og        (m)

m_o_p        (o)

an_t_        (t)

| mop | pig | hat | bed | duck |
|-----|-----|-----|-----|------|
| kid | net | log | rug | ant |

**On Your Own:**
Make up a short story using some of the words in the word list. Tell it to someone.

Spelling Grade 2—RBP3446

Read the words. Listen to the short <u>a</u> sound. Draw a picture next to each word.

happy

sad

glad

mad

bad

dad

rat

man

family

Read the words in the word list. Listen to the short <u>e</u> sound. Find all the words from the word list in the puzzle and circle them. Write each word.

| friend | pen | end | every | yes |
|--------|-----|-----|-------|-----|
| went | mess | send | cent | next |

```
p  f  r  a  h  s  l  e  m  y
k  l  f  d  q  s  v  x  k  e
d  l  r  n  o  e  t  b  u  s
r  c  i  e  l  m  x  v  j  i
o  e  e  s  v  f  e  o  t  v
e  n  n  g  c  j  n  n  o  g
j  t  d  y  t  h  e  n  d  u
e  h  p  d  r  w  p  m  l  r
n  o  e  k  k  e  d  n  e  q
k  a  n  y  r  e  v  e  l  i
```

_____  _____  _____

_____  _____  _____

_____  _____  _____

_____

Spelling Grade 2—RBP3446

Read the words in the word list. Listen to the short i sound. Using the secret code, write the missing letters of each word.

| win | listen | will | big | into |
| him | finish | grin | list | mitt |

| 1 | 2 | 3 | 4 | 5 | 6 | 7 | 8 | 9 | 10 | 11 | 12 | 13 | 14 |
|---|---|---|---|---|---|---|---|---|----|----|----|----|----|
| b | e | f | g | h | i | l | m | n | o | r | s | t | w |

**1.** <u>w</u> <u>i</u> <u>n</u>
   14  6  9

**2.** __ __ __
   1  6  4

**3.** __ __ __ __ __ __
   7  6  12  13  2  9

**4.** __ __ __ __
   4  11  6  9

**5.** __ __ __ __
   6  9  13  10

**6.** __ __ __ __
   14  6  7  7

**7.** __ __ __ __ __ __
   3  6  9  6  12  5

**8.** __ __ __
   5  6  8

**9.** __ __ __ __
   8  6  13  13

**10.** __ __ __ __
   7  6  12  13

**On Your Own:**
Use your detective skills and find some of these words in a magazine or newspaper.

## Short *o*

Read the words. Listen to the short <u>o</u> sound. Write a sentence using each word.

**1**. frog    <u>I saw a frog.</u>

**2**. song

**3**. on

**4**. not

**5**. off

**6**. hot

**7**. stop

**8**. gone

**9**. soggy

**On Your Own:**
Make a funny song using some of the words above.
Sing it to someone.

 Spelling Grade 2—RBP3446

Read the words in the word list. Listen to the short <u>u</u> sound. Copy and cut out the letters. Then put them together to make the words from the word list.

| A | B | C | D | E | F | G | H |
|---|---|---|---|---|---|---|---|
| I | J | K | L | M | N | O | P |
| Q | R | S | T | U | V | W | Y |

| | | | | |
|---|---|---|---|---|
| but | lucky | mud | fun | hungry |
| bug | stung | lunch | must | nut |

Read the words in the word list. Listen to the different long vowel sounds. Write a word from the word list in each space to complete the story.

1. Peter ate soup for <u>lunch</u> (hungry, lunch).

2. I was _____ (nut, stung) by a bee.

3. A spider is a type of _____ (bug, must).

4. Anna saw a chipmunk eat a _____ (lucky, nut).

5. I have _____ (fun, but) when I go swimming.

6. If you don't eat, you get _____ (hungry, mud).

# Long Vowels

Read the words in the word list. Listen to the different long vowel sounds. Write a word from the word list in each space to complete the story.

| | | | | |
|---|---|---|---|---|
| whale | float | tail | sea | bone |
| eel | bored | toad | alive | bite |

I went to the aquarium yesterday. I saw lots of cool things

_____

that live in the ___sea___. There was a huge

_____     _____

_____ with a big _____. I was scared

_____

that it might _____ me!  My favorite was the

_____     _____

_____, I wanted to _____ in the

_____

water with it. I liked the little green _____ too. It

_____

sat so still I thought it was dead, but it was _____,

_____

I thought I would feel _____ at the aquarium,

but I had fun.

9

Circle the word spelled correctly. Write the word and say it aloud. Listen to the long <u>a</u> sound.

1. rane    (rain)    raine    _____rain_____

2. make    maik    mak    _____

3. gaime    gaim    game    _____

4. day    dae    dai    _____

5. bak    baik    bake    _____

6. maybe    mabe    maby    _____

7. paint    paynt    piant    _____

8. clae    cla    clay    _____

9. sai    say    sae    _____

10. naym    name    nam    _____

Read the words. Listen to the long e sound. Copy and cut out the squares to make cards. Turn them face down. Pick a card and try to find its match. Write the word after you find each match.

| | |
|---|---|
| sleep | sleep |
| dream | dream |
| me | me |
| deep | deep |
| sheep | sheep |
| see | see |
| feel | feel |
| need | need |
| read | read |
| week | week |

1. _____

2. _____

3. _____

4. _____

5. _____

6. _____

7. _____

8. _____

9. _____

10. _____

Underline the misspelled word with your favorite colored marker. Write the word correctly. Read it aloud. Listen to the long i sound.

**1.** My <u>kyte</u> is in the sky. ___ kite ___

**2.** A dim is ten cents. ___

**3.** The winner gets a prise. ___

**4.** My favorite rede is the merry-go-round. ___

**5.** Someone very smart is wize. ___

**6.** I will invit them to my birthday party. ___

**7.** The water slyd is very fun. ___

**8.** I have been there twicee. ___

**9.** Have you played hyde-and-seek? ___

**10.** My friend is kend. ___

## Long *o*

Read the words in the word list. Listen to the long <u>o</u> sound. Unscramble each word and write it correctly.

| floor | store | row | sold | open |
|-------|-------|------|------|------|
| close | so | more | door | load |

**1.** os     so

**2.** odls _____

**3.** ordo _____

**4.** owr _____

**5.** rfool _____

**6.** nepo _____

**7.** odla _____

**8.** rmoe _____

**9.** roset _____

**10.** socel _____

    Spelling Grade 2—RBP3446

Read the words in the word list. Listen to the long _u_ sound. Use the words from the word list to complete the sentences. Use each word once.

| | | | | |
|---|---|---|---|---|
| school | ruler | glue | use | pool |
| rules | tool | noon | too | tune |

**1.** I have a _ruler_ in my desk at _____.

**2.** I eat lunch at _____.

**3.** I _____ the diving board at the _____.

**4.** _____ is very sticky.

**5.** Hum the _____ of the song.

**6.** She likes to read. I like to read, _____.

**7.** A hammer is a _____.

**8.** I have to obey all the _____.

# Silent e and Long Vowel Sounds

When an <u>e</u> is added to the end of a word, the short vowel sound becomes a long vowel sound. Read the words and listen to the short vowel sounds. Add an <u>e</u> to the end of each word and write the new words. Read the new words aloud and listen to the long vowel sounds.

| hat | hop | mad | at | cut | dim |
|-----|-----|------|-----|------|------|
| hate | hope | made | ate | cute | dime |

**1**. hat _____ e _____ _____ hate _____

**2**. hop _____ _____

**3**. mad _____ _____

**4**. at _____ _____

**5**. cut _____ _____

**6**. dim _____ _____

Think of another word with a short vowel sound. Add an <u>e</u> and write the new word.

**7**. _____ _____ _____

# *ch* and *sh*

Read each word in the word list. Listen to the <u>ch</u> and <u>sh</u> sounds.

| | | | | | |
|---|---|---|---|---|---|
| ship | fish | wash | she | chin | each |
| much | child | shut | should | such | beach |

Write the words that begin with the <u>sh</u> sound.

Write the words that begin with the <u>ch</u> sound.

Write the words that end with the <u>sh</u> sound.

Write the words that end with the <u>ch</u> sound.

# *wh* Words

Read the words in the word list. Listen to the <u>wh</u> sounds. A newspaper wants to interview you for a story. Answer the questions below to help them write the story.

| who | what | when | where | why |
|-----|------|------|-------|-----|
| while | which | whose | whom | whole |

1. Who is your teacher? _____

2. What is your favorite color? _____

3. When is your birthday? _____

4. Where are you from? _____

5. Why do you like school? _____

Write the <u>wh</u> in front of each word to finish the words from the word list.

6. _____ ile

7. _____ ich

8. _____ ole

9. _____ om

10. _____ ose

# *th* Words

Read the words in the word list. Listen to the <u>th</u> sounds. Follow the directions and use the map to trace your way from school to the ice cream shop.

| | | | | |
|---|---|---|---|---|
| this | that | them | thank | thin |
| north | south | path | then | with |

## Directions:

1. Color the house in the bottom left corner.
2. Draw a line north until you reach the stop sign.
3. Continue drawing the same path until you reach a group of friends. Take them with you as you turn right.
4. Then, keep going right until you reach a thin sign.
5. Draw a line south until you reach the ice cream shop.

Be sure to say thank you for the ice cream!

Read the words in the word list. Listen to the <u>k</u> sound that is made by <u>c</u>, <u>k</u>, and <u>ck</u>. Fill in the missing letters to make the words in the word list.

| | | | | |
|---|---|---|---|---|
| bark | rock | duck | pick | come |
| like | hike | think | camp | cut |

1. _____ u t

2. b _____ _____ k

3. _____ a m _____

4. r o _____ _____

5. t h i _____ _____

K sounds are kind of cool!

6. _____ u _____ k

7. h _____ _____ e

8. p _____ c _____

9. li _____ _____

10. _____ _____ m e

# Blends with *r—cr, dr, fr, gr,* and *tr*

Read the words in the word list. Listen to the sounds made with the letter <u>r</u> in each word, like <u>cr</u>, <u>dr</u>, <u>fr</u>, <u>gr</u>, and <u>tr</u>. Complete the I Spy statements with words from the word list.

| trash | tree | breeze | train | cry | pretty |
| brother | great | front | free | trip | |

**1.** I SPY a garbage bag full of unwanted things.

I SPY _trash_.

**2.** I SPY a boy with a sister.

I SPY a _____.

**3.** I SPY some huge cars hooked together on a track.

I SPY a _____.

**4.** I SPY a small wind blowing our hair.

I SPY a _____.

**5.** I SPY a tall, brown trunk with brown branches and green leaves.

I SPY a _____.

Read the words in the word list. Listen to the sounds made with the letter l in each word, like cl, sl, fl, and pl. Alphabetize the groups of words below.

| planet | slow | slam | flew | close | plane |
|--------|------|------|------|-------|-------|
| clock | please | glass | glove | blast | |

glass, slow, planet

1. glass

2. planet

3. slow

clock, please, close

1. _____

2. _____

3. _____

slam, flew, glove

1. _____

2. _____

3. _____

plane, blast, slow

1. _____

2. _____

3. _____

**On Your Own:**
5, 4, 3, 2, 1 . . . blastoff! Write or tell someone about a trip to space you want to take. Use words that have cl, sl, fl, and pl sounds.

# Blends with s—*sk, sm, sn, sp, st,* and *sw*

Read the words in the word list. Listen to the sounds made with the letter s in each word, like <u>sk</u>, <u>sm</u>, <u>sn</u>, <u>sp</u>, <u>st</u>, and <u>sw</u>. Write the correct word from the word list in the blanks.

| | | | | | |
|---|---|---|---|---|---|
| slick | sled | sleet | snow | ski | smile |
| sport | spark | spin | slide | stop | swing |

1. I am found at a park. You sit on me and go back and forth. I can go really high. I am a swing.

2. I am basketball, baseball, tennis, hockey, or bowling. I am a _____.

3. I am on your face. I am always with you when you're happy. I am a _____.

4. I am at a park. You have fun going down me. I am a _____.

5. I am white and flaky. You play with me when it is cold outside. I am _____.

6. I am something that you use to travel down a snowy hill. I am a _____.

# Blends with r—*str, spr,* and *thr*

Read the words in the word list. Listen to the sounds made with the letter r in each word, like str, spr, and thr. Write str, spr, or thr to complete each word.

| | | | | |
|---|---|---|---|---|
| spring | stream | street | throw | straw |
| strong | spray | through | straight | sprout |

**1.** <u>S p r</u> ing is a season that comes before summer.

**2.** Draw a __ __ __ aight line.

**3.** How far can you __ __ __ow a football?

**4.** He carried that heavy box. He is very __ __ __ong.

**5.** The flowers begin to __ __ __out in the spring.

**6.** I like to drink using a __ __ __aw.

**7.** We play near the __ __ __eam.

**8.** I hold my breath when I drive __ __ __ough a tunnel.

**9.** My sister helps __ __ __ay the plants with water.

**10.** My best friend lives across the __ __ __eet from me.

Spelling Grade 2—RBP3446

# kn and wr

Read the words in the word list. Listen to the <u>kn</u> and <u>wr</u> sounds. Complete the knock-knock joke below with words from the word list.

| | | | | |
|---|---|---|---|---|
| knock | know | knife | write | knot |
| wrap | wrong | wrist | knee | |

1. Knock-__knock__, Who's there? Knee!

_____

_____ who? Knee-d you ask?

Use a favorite color to circle the <u>kn</u> and <u>wr</u> sounds in the words below. Write each word.

2. know  _____

3. wrap  _____

4. wrist  _____

5. knife  _____

6. write  _____

7. knot  _____

8. wrong  _____

# *un* and *re*

Read the words in the word list. Notice they all begin with the prefixes <u>un</u> and <u>re</u>. <u>Un</u> at the beginning of a word means "not." <u>Re</u> at the beginning of a word means "again." Write the correct word in the spaces.

| | | | | |
|---|---|---|---|---|
| refill | uneven | unsafe | undo | rename |
| redo | unsure | reset | retell | unsaid |

**1.** I fill the glass with milk again.  _refill_

**2.** I was not sure what to do.  _____

**3.** The old playground was not safe.  _____

**4.** Grandpa will tell the story again.  _____

**5.** She will do the homework again.  _____

Write the words in the word list that were not used above. Underline the prefix <u>re</u> in blue and the prefix <u>un</u> in red.

**6.**  _____        **9.**  _____

**7.**  _____        **10.**  _____

**8.**  _____

Spelling Grade 2—RBP3446

# The *s* Sound with the Letter *c*

Read the words in the word list. Listen to the s sound made with the letter c in each word. Write the correct words from the word list to solve the puzzle.

| | | | | | |
|---|---|---|---|---|---|
| circle | city | cent | nice | circus | race |
| place | fence | chance | face | mice | |

**Across**

1. Three blind _____ mice _____.

3. This is a shape. _____

5. Opposite of <u>mean</u>. _____

**Down**

2. Animals do tricks at the _____.

4. This is one penny. _____

6. New York is a _____.

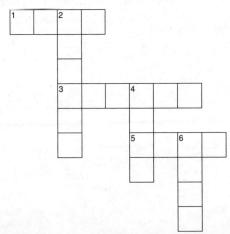

©RBP Books

# The *j* Sound with the Letter *g*

Read the words in the word list. Listen to the j sound that is made with the letter g in each word. Fill in the missing letters to make the words from the word list.

| | | | | |
|---|---|---|---|---|
| bridge | judge | change | large | gentle |
| giant | germ | age | cage | huge |

**1.** g __e__ __r__ m

**2.** ___ ___ r g e

**3.** j u d ___ ___

**4.** ___ e n t l ___

**5.** a ___ ___

**6.** c h a n ___ ___

**7.** b r i ___ ___ e

**8.** c ___ ___ e

**9.** h u ___ ___

**10.** ___ i a n ___

Spelling is JUST GREAT!

Read the words in the word list. Listen to the two different sounds made by the letters oo. In column 1, write the words from the list with the oo sound that you hear in soon. In column 2, write the words from the list with the oo sound that you hear in look.

| spoon | food | look | cook | soon |
| room | tooth | good | broom | book |

## Column 1

soon

## Column 2

look

## oa and o

Read the words in the word list. Listen to the sound that is made by <u>oa</u> and <u>o</u>. Write a word from the word list next to each clue. Use the numbers to break the code.

| | | | | | |
|---|---|---|---|---|---|
| toad | boat | coat | cold | old | soap |
| low | hold | road | row | float | |

1. Opposite of hot. <u>c</u> <u>o</u> <u>l</u> <u>d</u>
        8

2. Opposite of high. __ __ __
           5

3. Opposite of young. __ __ __
          11

Wow! This looks like quite a puzzle!

4. Use this to clean with. __ __ __ __
         7

5. Wear this when it's cold outside. __ __ __ __
               1

6. Sit in this when fishing. __ __ __ __
           4

7. Opposite of sink. __ __ __ __ __
          6

8. Cars drive on this. __ __ __ __
        10

Yeah, but we can solve it!

9. This lives in a pond. __ __ __ __
        3

10. Do this to move a boat. __ __ __
         9

11. To carry something. __ __ __ __
      2

__ __ __ __  __ __ __  __ __ __ __!
1 2 3 4  5 6 7  8 9 10 11

Spelling Grade 2—RBP3446

# *ou* and *ow*

Read the words in the word list. Listen to the sound that is made by <u>ou</u> and <u>ow</u>. Then finish writing this e-mail to a friend. Use the word list to help you fill in the blanks.

| | | | | | |
|---|---|---|---|---|---|
| cloud | outside | loud | sound | town | crowd |
| house | now | out | about | around | |

Hi!

I have to tell you ab_____t my day today. It was a nice

day. There was only one cl_____d in the sky, so my

mom and I went out_____. We went to t_____n.

Suddenly I heard a l_____d bang. The s_____nd

was so loud that a big cr_____ of people looked

ar_____ to see what happened. N_____w I'm back

safe in my h_____e. I'm glad. I don't want to go

back o_____t for a while.

Bye

---

30

# *all*, *au*, and *aw*

Read the words in the word list. Listen to the sound that is made by <u>all</u>, <u>au</u>, and <u>aw</u>. Unscramble each word and write it correctly.

| | | | | | |
|---|---|---|---|---|---|
| small | fall | draw | saw | water | walk |
| talk | cause | taught | all | lawn | |

**1.** darw    draw

**2.** aws

**3.** waln

**4.** wrate

**5.** llaf

**6.** smlla

**7.** tghuat

**8.** ecaus

**9.** lal

**10.** ktal

**11.** kalw

31

# Double Letters

Read the words in the word list. Listen to the sound that is made by two of the same letter next to each other. Help make a map of a zoo. Write the correct word from the word list and draw a picture of it.

| | | | | |
|---|---|---|---|---|
| zoo | goose | deer | rabbit | parrot |
| rooster | raccoon | moose | gorilla | balloon |

## Zoo Map

g_____se    b_____n    m_____se

ra_____n    r_____it    pa_____t

go_____a    d_____r    r_____ter

Read the words in the word list. Listen to the sound that is made by <u>ai</u>, <u>ay</u>, and <u>eigh</u>. Find and circle all the words you can from the word list in the puzzle. The words may go up and down or sideways.

| | | | | |
|---|---|---|---|---|
| pay | weigh | stay | faint | may |
| raise | play | tail | snail | sleigh |

```
p q v l g f d q y e
x v t j i s i t m u
d r p a l p n q l h
l j d e i n c g i d
f s i e x l r m a y
m g t s l h l t n s
h c r a i s e w s a
u z p x y k w i z x
g p z s o k t g e r
p y a l p l y u d l
```

Write the three words from the word list that you did NOT find in the word search.

_____          _____

**1.** f _____ nt          **2.** p _____ y

_____

**3.** we _____

Word searches are my favorite!

# ee and ea

Circle the word spelled correctly. Write the word and say it aloud. Listen to the sounds made by <u>ee</u> and <u>ea</u>.

| | | | | |
|---|---|---|---|---|
| year | deer | fear | clear | near |
| ear | reach | seed | lead | bee |

1. lode    (lead)    leed    _lead_

2. year    yeer    yer    _____

3. sead    sede    seed    _____

4. deer    der    deor    _____

5. reech    reac    reach    _____

6. fear    feer    fer    _____

7. ear    eer    eor    _____

8. kleer    cleer    clear    _____

9. bea    bee    bao    _____

10. meer    near    neer    _____

Read the words on the tic-tac-toe board. Listen to the sound that is made by <u>ar</u>. Play tic-tac-toe either alone or with someone you know. Draw a circle around or put an X through the words. After a word is chosen, write the word on a line below.

| | | |
|:---:|:---:|:---:|
| car | hard | arm |
| dark | yard | start |
| star | park | far |

1. _____

2. _____

3. _____

4. _____

5. _____

6. _____

7. _____

8. _____

9. _____

Read the words in the word list. Listen to the sound that is made by <u>er</u>, <u>ear</u>, <u>ir</u>, <u>or</u>, and <u>ur</u>. Choose the correct word to complete each sentence.

| girl | work | dirt | shirt | her | turn |
|------|------|------|-------|-----|------|
| learn | heard | burn | fern | worm | |

**1.** I like to read so I can (learn) her).

**2.** Have you (heard, worm) the song on the radio?

**3.** He is wearing a blue (work, shirt) today.

**4.** She is not a boy. She is a (heard, girl).

**5.** I like (her, turn) shoes.

**6.** The (worm, heard) outside likes the (her, dirt).

**7.** I help Dad (shirt, turn) the wheel of the car.

**8.** He has a sore (burn, work).

**9.** The (her, fern) is a pretty plant.

**10.** Grandma likes to (work, girl) in her garden.

Read the words. Listen to the sound that is made by
<u>or</u> and <u>our</u>. Write a short sentence using each word.

1. morning ___I like morning.___

2. for _____

3. corn _____

4. horse _____

5. fork _____

6. your _____

7. corner _____

8. order _____

9. horn _____

## *oo, ou,* and *u*

Read the words in the word list. Listen to the sounds that are made by <u>oo</u>, <u>ou</u>, and <u>u</u>. Fill in the missing vowels to complete the words from the word list. Color the vowels one color and the consonants another.

| | | | | | |
|---|---|---|---|---|---|
| foot | put | push | took | full | hook |
| pull | brook | stood | could | would | |

1. f <u>**o**</u> <u>**o**</u> t

2. w __ __ ld

3. p __ t

4. c __ __ ld

5. p __ sh

6. st __ __ d

7. t __ __ k

8. br __ __ k

9. h __ __ k

10. f __ ll

11. p __ ll

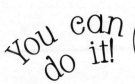

www.summerbridgeactivities.com

©RBP Books

## *oi* and *oy*

Read the words in the word list. Listen to the same sound that is made by <u>oi</u> and <u>oy</u>. Write the correct word from the word list in the spaces below.

| | | | | |
|---|---|---|---|---|
| toy | enjoy | boy | coin | noise |
| annoy | joy | spoil | voice | join |

1. Tom's brother says I ___annoy___ him.

2. My dad has a _____ collection.

3. I love going to the _____ store.

4. He is not a girl. He is a _____ .

5. My friend has a good singing _____ .

6. I want to _____ the club.

7. If you don't put the milk away, it will _____ .

8. We _____ hiking.

9. There is a lot of _____ in the city.

Read the words in the word list. Listen to the <u>mp</u> and <u>nd</u> sounds at the end of each word. Write the words from the word list. Circle all the <u>mp</u> endings and underline all the <u>nd</u> endings.

| | | | | |
|---|---|---|---|---|
| jump | stand | hand | thump | bump |
| stomp | ramp | band | around | limp |

1. jump

2. _____

3. _____

4. _____

5. _____

6. _____

7. _____

8. _____

9. _____

10. _____

Say each word aloud again. This time, jump once when you say an <u>mp</u> word and turn around once when you say an <u>nd</u> word.

Read the words in the word list. Listen to the <u>nk</u> and <u>nt</u> sounds at the end of each word. Write each word from the word list in the correct blank space. Connect all the dots.

| ink | bank | shrink | think | link | sank |
| hint | sink | different | drink | print | point |

1. hi _nt_____

2. diff _____

3. b _____k

4. in _____

5. shr_____

6. si _____

7. sa _____

8. thi _____

9. po _____t

10. dr _____

1. 2. 3. 4. 5. 6. 7. 8. 9. 10

Spelling Grade 2—RBP3446

Read the words in the word list. Listen to the <u>lf</u>, <u>lm</u>, <u>lp</u>, and <u>lt</u> sounds at the end of each word. Match the beginning of each word from the word list with its correct ending. Write each word after the match is made.

| belt | help | felt | gulp | shelf |
| myself | halt | quilt | elf | calm |

be      lf

ca      lt

he      lf

e      lt

fe      lm

qui      lt

gu      lf

ha      lt

she      lp

myse      lp

belt

Read the words in the word list. Listen to the <u>sk</u>, <u>sp</u>, and <u>st</u> sounds at the beginning or end of each word. Circle the correct words from the word list to complete the story.

| | | | | |
|---|---|---|---|---|
| last | past | fast | gasp | dust |
| forest | ask | step | stump | skunk |

## My Visit to the Forest

(Fast, Last) night I went into a dark (ask, forest). I saw a (skunk, step) run (last, past) me. It ran so (fast, forest)! I was so surprised that I let out a (gasp, dust). It stopped and sat on a tree (dust, stump). I took one (step, past) toward it. I was about to (forest, ask) his name, but suddenly . . .

Finish the story using two more <u>sk</u>, <u>sp</u>, or <u>st</u> words.

Read the words in the word list. Listen to the <u>or</u>, <u>er</u>, and <u>ar</u> sounds at the end of each word. Add an <u>or</u>, <u>er</u>, or <u>ar</u> ending to each of the words to make a word from the word list.

| doctor | lawyer | teacher | sailor | dancer |
|--------|--------|---------|--------|--------|
| farmer | actor | singer | officer | dollar |

**1.** d o c t **o**   **r**

**2.** d o l l __ __

**3.** t e a c h __ __

**4.** s i n g __ __

**5.** f a r m __ __

**6.** l a w y __ __

**7.** s a i l __ __

**8.** d a n c __ __

**9.** a c t __ __

**10.** o f f i c __ __

Sing a song of r endings!

**11.** What do you want to be when you grow up?

_____

# *y* Sounds

Read the words in the word list. Listen to the two different sounds the _y_ makes. Write the words from the word list in the column with the same sounds.

| | | | | | |
|---|---|---|---|---|---|
| sky | fly | happy | by | many | dry |
| hardly | candy | healthy | penny | my | |

y (long _i_ sound)          y (long _e_ sound)

sky                         candy

          Spelling Grade 2—RBP3446

# Double Letters

Read the words in the word list. Listen to the single sound made from two of the same letter next to each other in each word. Match the beginning of each word from the word list with its correct ll, ss, dd, or ff ending. Write each word after the match is made.

| ball | yell | toss | grass | pass | off |
|------|------|------|-------|------|-----|
| well | call | miss | mitt | hill | add |

ba     ll   _____

a      ll   _____

ye     ss   _____

hi     ss   _____

to     ll   _____

mi     dd   _____

Do the same with the next group of words.

gra    tt   _____

ca     ss   _____

pa     ll   _____

we     ff   _____

o      ll   _____

mi     ss   _____

# Plurals—*s* and *es*

Read the words in the word list. Fill in the sentence with the correct word from the word list. The s and es endings are added to the words to make them plural. Circle the s and es endings in each word.

| | | |
|---|---|---|
| wishes | boxes | toads |
| matches | bugs | crashes |

**1.** The genie granted him three ___wish(es)___ .

**2.** She can carry two _____ .

**3.** Five _____ jumped by the pond.

**4.** Grandpa used two _____ to start the fire.

**5.** There are ten _____ in his bug jar.

**6.** There were three car _____ yesterday.

# ed and *ing*

Read the words in the word list. Listen to the ed and ing sounds at the end of each word. Write the correct word from the word list in the spaces below. Pay close attention when adding or taking away letters before adding the ed and ing endings.

hopped   swinging   running   waved   played   smiling

**1.** hop   +   ed   =   _hopped_

**2.** swing +   ing   =   _____

**3.** run   +   ing   =   _____

**4.** wave +   ed   =   _____

**5.** play   +   ed   =   _____

**6.** smile +   ing   =   _____

# *er* and *est*

Read the words in the word list. Listen to the <u>er</u> and <u>est</u> endings of each word. Fill in the chart below with words from the word list. Notice when letters must be added or taken away from the word before <u>er</u> or <u>est</u> is added.

| bigger | funnier | messiest |
|--------|---------|----------|
| quicker | nicest | widest |

| Base Word | + er/est | New Word |
|-----------|----------|----------|
| big | er | bigger |
| funny | er | |
| messy | est | |
| quick | er | |
| nice | est | |
| wide | est | |

Spelling Grade 2—RBP3446

Read the words in the word list. Listen to the sound that is made from <u>air</u> and <u>are</u>. Write the correct word from the word list to complete each sentence.

| | | | | |
|---|---|---|---|---|
| hair | care | pair | dare | stairs |
| chair | stare | share | air | scare |

1. She has long ___hair___.

2. We have a _____ of eyes.

3. I double _____ you to do that!

4. Sit in the _____.

5. Will you _____ with me?

6. Don't _____ me on Halloween.

7. It isn't nice to _____.

8. I have to climb up the _____.

9. I want to go outside for some fresh _____.

10. My teacher does _____ about me.

# Words That End in *le*

Read the words in the word list. Listen to the sound <u>le</u> makes at the end of each word. Add an <u>le</u> to the end of the words and write the new words.

| | | | | |
|---|---|---|---|---|
| able | bubble | table | trouble | little |
| tickle | bottle | rattle | puzzle | wiggle |

**1**. ab _le_ _able_

**2**. wigg _____ _____

**3**. bubb _____ _____

**4**. puzz _____ _____

**5**. tab _____ _____

**6**. ratt _____ _____

**7**. troub _____ _____

**8**. tick _____ _____

**9**. bott _____ _____

**10**. litt _____ _____

# *ies* and *ied*

Read the words in the word list. Listen to the different sounds made from the <u>ies</u> and <u>ied</u> endings. Underline the <u>ies</u> or <u>ied</u> ending. Write the word.

| flies | skies | tried | cried | cherries |
|-------|-------|-------|-------|----------|
| babies | ladies | carries | pies | fried |

1. fl<u>ies</u>       fl<u>ies</u>

2. skies       _____

3. carries     _____

4. tried       _____

5. cried       _____

6. cherries    _____

7. babies      _____

8. ladies      _____

9. pies        _____

10. fried      _____

Read each word in the word list. Listen to how the words change when they are made plural and the <u>f</u> changes to a <u>v</u>. Copy and cut the squares to make cards. Turn them all face down and try to find the plural and its match. Write the plural of the word after you find each match.

| | |
|---|---|
| life | lives |
| leaf | leaves |
| shelf | shelves |
| calf | calves |
| wife | wives |
| half | halves |

**1**. life _____

**2**. leaf _____

**3**. shelf _____

**4**. calf _____

**5**. wife _____

**6**. half _____

# *ph* and *gh*

Read the words in the word list. Listen to the sounds made by <u>ph</u> and <u>gh</u>. Write <u>ph</u> or <u>gh</u> in the spaces to complete each word from the word list. Connect all the dots.

| phone | graph | laugh | tough | photo |
|-------|-------|-------|-------|-------|
| phrase | enough | rough | cough | trough |

**1.** _____ph_____ one

**2.** _____ oto

**3.** gra _____

**4.** enou _____

**5.** trou _____

**6.** _____ rase

**7.** rou _____

**8.** lau _____

**9.** cou _____

**10.** tou _____

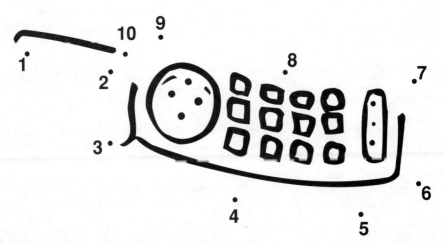

## ew, oe, and ou

Read the words in the word list. Listen to the sound that is made from <u>ew</u>, <u>oe</u>, and <u>ou</u>. Copy the letters. Cut them out and put them together to make the words in the word list.

| A | B | C | D | E | F | G | H |
|---|---|---|---|---|---|---|---|
| I | J | K | L | M | N | O | P |
| Q | R | S | T | U | V | W | X |
| Y | Z | | | | | | |

| | | | | |
|---|---|---|---|---|
| you | through | group | chew | shoe |
| dew | new | drew | stew | few |

Choose the correct word to complete each sentence.

1. I lost my ___shoe___. (shoe, few)

2. Do you like my _____ game? (you, new)

3. Don't _____ with your mouth open. (shoe, chew)

4. She _____ me a picture. (clue, drew)

5. There are only a _____ cookies left. (drew, few)

55

# Homonyms

Read the words in the word list. Pay attention to how words can sound the same but can be spelled differently and mean different things. Circle the word that will make the sentence correct.

| | | | | |
|---|---|---|---|---|
| sea | their | son | red | buy |
| peace | mail | see | there | sun |
| read | by | piece | male | |

**1.** Do you have a (piece, peace) of paper?

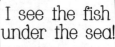
I see the fish under the sea!

**2.** I want to (male, mail) a letter.

**3.** Fish live in the (see, sea).

**4.** That father has a (sun, son).

**5.** My favorite color is (read, red).

**6.** He is going to (buy, by) that for her.

**7.** Are we (there, their) yet?

# Contractions

Read the words in the word list. Pay attention to what happens to letters when a contraction is made. Write the contraction of the underlined words to make the same sentence.

| | | | | |
|---|---|---|---|---|
| you're | I'll | don't | isn't | it's |
| I'm | can't | we're | he'd | she'll |

1. <u>I am</u> eight years old.

   I'm eight years old.

2. <u>It is</u> good.

   _____ good.

3. <u>She will</u> be happy.

   _____ be happy.

4. <u>You are</u> nice.

   _____ nice.

5. <u>Do not</u> touch!

   _____ touch!

6. <u>We are</u> best friends.

   _____ best friends.

7. I <u>can not</u> go.

   I _____ go.

8. <u>I will</u> call you.

   _____ call you.

9. <u>He would</u> come.

   _____ come.

10. That <u>is not</u> funny.

    That _____ funny.

© RBP Books

Spelling Grade 2—RBP3446

# Compound Words

Read the words in the word box. See how two words put together become a new word. Fill in the blanks using the correct words and parts of words from the word list.

| | | | |
|---|---|---|---|
| cupcake | birthday | inside | myself |
| something | girlfriend | anyone | weekend |

**1.** cup + cake = _cupcake_

**2.** some + _____ = something

**3.** any + _____ = anyone

**4.** week + end = _____

**5.** _____ + day = birthday

**6.** girl + _____ = girlfriend

**7.** in + side = _____

**8.** _____ + self = myself

www.summerbridgeactivities.com   © RBP Books

# Rhyming Words

Read the words in the word box. Listen to the words that rhyme with each other. Write the word that rhymes with the underlined word to complete the sentences.

| long | hat | mouse | hen | healthy |
|------|-----|-------|-----|---------|
| song | mat | house | pen | wealthy |

**1.** There is a <u>hat</u> under the _____ mat _____.

**2.** Do you see the <u>hen</u> in a _____?

**3.** I'm happy to be <u>healthy</u>, _____ and wise.

**4.** There is a _____ in my <u>house</u>.

**5.** That <u>song</u> is very _____.

Think of two more words that rhyme. Write a silly sentence using the words.

_____

_____

_____

_____

_____

_____

# Ordinal Number Words

Read the number words in the word list. Write who is in which place in the race.

| first | second | third | fourth | fifth |
|-------|--------|-------|--------|-------|
| sixth | seventh | eighth | ninth | tenth |

**Allie** | **Matt** | **Grayson** | **Denise** | **Rob** | **Lori** | **Tanner**

**Start**                                                 **Finish Line**

1. _Allie_____ is in last place.

2. Rob is in _____ place.

3. Matt is in _____ place.

4. _____ is in second place.

5. Denise is in _____ place.

6. Lori is in _____ place.

7. Grayson is in _____ place.

8. Tanner is in _____ place.

# Days of the Week

Read the days of the week words in the word list. Look at the weather forecast and complete the sentences. Use the words from the word list.

| | | | |
|---|---|---|---|
| Sunday | Monday | Tuesday | Wednesday |
| Week | Thursday | Friday | Saturday |

**Monday** **Tuesday** **Wednesday** **Thursday** **Friday** **Saturday**

1. On _____Thursday_____ it will be _____ .

2. _____ will be _____ .

3. It will _____ on _____ ,

4. On _____ it will be _____ .

5. _____ will be _____ .

6. It will be _____ on _____ ,

7. There are seven days in one _____ ,

8. My favorite day of the week is _____ ,

## Spelling Sleuth

You are a spelling sleuth (slooth). A sleuth is a detective. You are working on the case of the word thief. The thief has left many clues behind. The first one is on this page. Your job is to collect the clues and put them together to find the thief.

### Crime:
A dog has disappeared from an empty lot on Barking Lane.

### Evidence:
The thief left a note under a rock. The note said,
"The dog will be returned once I've got the letters I need.

Sincerely,
Mr. X"

### Witness Report:
A woman saw three people in the lot before the dog was missing: a boy on a bike, a man in a trench coat wearing a hat, and a woman carrying an umbrella.

### Find the Clues:
Read the note from the thief.
Which person is the most likely suspect?
How do you know?

_____

_____

_____

_____

_____

## Spelling Sleuth

### Second Witness Report:

A second witness reported that the man was wearing a hat, but she could not remember the exact color. She did say that the color had a short vowel in its name.

### Find the Clues:

List all the colors with a short vowel sound you can think of.

Colors?

## Spelling Sleuth

### Crime:
The grocery store has been robbed!
Letters from canned food labels have disappeared. No one can tell what is inside the cans without opening them.

### Evidence:
An empty can of stew was found in the mess. It had a note tucked inside that said "Collecting letters is hard work, and the dog was hungry. Here's fifty cents to pay for the food I ate. Thanks, X

P.S.   The labels all had letters I could use. Sorry about the mess."

### Find the Clues:
Some names from the food cans can be found below. To figure out what letters the thief has taken, fill in the missing letters to finish each word.

1. __ or __

2. __ ear __

3. __ __ c __ les

4. st __ __ __ __ beans

5. __ ea __ __ es

6. __ __ __ r __ ies

7. s __ __ __ sh

8. cr __ shed __ __ __ __ __ pple

9. sp __ ced __ __ __ __ kin

## Spelling Sleuth

### Crime:

The highways are backed up for miles. The drivers don't knows where they are going. All of the north and south signs have disappeared. The word thief has struck again. There is no way for anyone to get off the highway without some directions.

Look at the map below. Give directions to each car for the best exit off the highway. Make sure to tell the drivers to drive north or south.

Car A: Drive south to exit 4.

Car B:

Car C:

Car D:

Car E:

List eight words the word thief could be making with the letters <u>th</u> in them.

_____     _____

_____     _____

_____     _____

_____     _____

## Spelling Sleuth

A spelling sleuth has to ask lots of questions to solve a mystery. Many question words begin with the letters <u>wh</u>. List as many <u>wh</u> question words as you can.

_____

_____

_____

_____

_____

_____

_____

© RBP Books

## Spelling Sleuth

### Crime:

A new movie is playing at the Picture Plex. In the end credits, the actors' names were there, but the parts they played were not!

### Find the Clues:

Read what each actor did in the movie. Write down the part each actor played to discover the missing words. What do the words have in common?

Tilly O'Toole: taught school in the first scene, so she played the part of the t __ __ __ __ __ __ .

Oliver Otley: was a policeman who chased after the criminals. He played the part of the o __ __ __ __ __ __ .

Lenny Lester: defended the criminal in court, so he played the part of the l __ __ __ __ __ .

Fred Forrest: milked the cows in the pasture by the schoolhouse. He played the part of the f __ __ __ __ __ .

Sid Samuel: was sailing in his boat when he found the thief. He played the part of the s __ __ __ __ __ .

Ben Brennan: owned the bank where the criminal had taken some money. He was the b __ __ __ __ __ .

Donna Delham: worked in a hospital where the criminal was taken. She played the part of the d __ __ __ __ __ .

Selia Santana: sang the song that played at the end of the movie. She was the s __ __ __ __ __ .

## Spelling Sleuth

### Crime:
While visiting the zoo, several families noticed that signs were missing from the animals' cages.

### Evidence:
A note taped to the gatepost read: "All the signs missing are the kinds of words needed for my collection. It was lots of fun to see so many different kinds of animals in one place. Sincerely, X"

### Find the Clues:
The animals pictured below are the ones whose names were found missing. Write each animal's name. Then look for what the names have in common.

What do the names have in common?

## Spelling Sleuth

### Evidence:
You've just received a letter with no return address and no stamp. (It must have been hand delivered.)

You open it and find a scrambled message inside. There is a hint at the bottom of the letter. It says: "All of the scrambled words have <u>ph</u> and <u>gh</u> in them. It may seem tou<u>gh</u>, but I'm sure a smart sleuth like you can solve the <u>ph</u>rases."

### Find the Clues:
Unscramble the words below to see what the letter says. (Bonus: You think the letter is a fake. Why?)

Meet me at the (aughLing) (ouhgTr) Restaurant to talk about the money I want for returning the dog.

A (ocuhgnig) voice on the (enohp) will give you (gouehn) information to (ragph) directions to the restaurant. When you meet me there, I will be carrying a (otoph) of the missing dog.     Signed, Ex

69

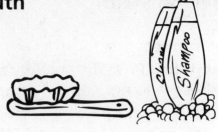

## Spelling Sleuth

**Critical Thinking Skills**

### Crime:
There is a problem at the beauty salon downtown. The labels on the bottles are missing words. A hairdresser shows you the bottles of shampoo, coloring, perm solution, and conditioner that are left.

### Find the Clues:
Can you fill in the missing words on the bottles and find a way to tell what is in each bottle?

Explain to the hairdresser how to figure out what is in each bottle: _____

_____

## Spelling Sleuth

Sometimes detectives must think in a new way in order to fit clues together. Think of other spellings for the underlined sounds in the words below. Write words with the new spellings for the same sounds next to each word. Draw a line under the sounds.

**Example:**

**1.** sh<u>oe</u>—f<u>ew</u>, thr<u>ough</u>, cl<u>ue</u>

**2.** st<u>aff</u>—

**3.** st<u>are</u>—

**4.** t<u>oy</u>—

**5.** c<u>oo</u>k—

**6.** cl<u>ou</u>d—

**7.** l<u>ear</u>n—

**8.** g<u>ear</u>—

**9.** sl<u>eigh</u>—

**10.** w<u>a</u>lk—

71

## Spelling Sleuth

### Crime:
The word thief has struck again. Letters were taken from a sign at the aquarium downtown. A note was left in their place.

### Evidence:
The note reads, "I've gone somewhere with a name that tells what the missing letters have in common.

Signed, X"

### Find the Clues:
The sign now says,

"Come and s__ __ the wh__les from the s__ __ d__ve

and fl__ __t in our h__ge pool!"

Can you fill in the missing letters to find out what the sounds have in common?

Circle the place where the word thief has gone.

Long Island

Blending Boardwalk

Short's Shrimp Shack

Silent Street

72

# Spelling Sleuth

Fill in the missing half of the compound words on this map of Long Island. Then follow the clues in order to find the missing dog.

## Clues:

_____walk, camp_____, _____grounds, side_____, flower_____, _____market, down_____, free_____, _____house, _____port

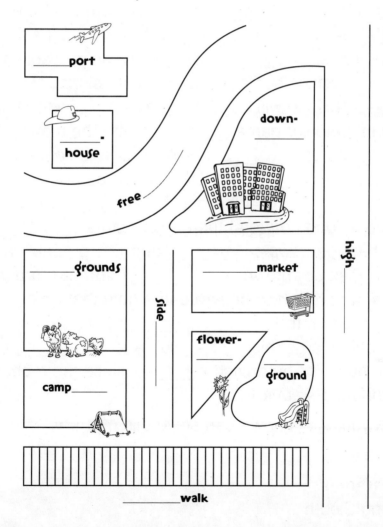

## Spelling Sleuth

**Critical Thinking Skills**

In order to find the thief you must write a letter to the Senior Sleuth, your boss. You will prove that you have the clues you need to catch the thief. Write the word for each number in ( ), and fill in the missing words in the clues. Look at the pages you've completed for help with the answers.

Dear Sir,

Listed below are the clues I have collected to help catch the word thief. ____**First**____ (1st), the word thief will probably be seen with a _____ stolen from the lot on Barking Lane. _____(2nd), the thief is probably a _____ since some of his notes are signed "Mr. X." _____(3rd), he will be wearing a _____ with a short vowel in the color name. _____ (4th), he may be carrying lots of _____, like A, B, C, and some words in his pockets. _____ (5th), he will be on _____ Island. _____ (6th), he may have _____ on him from the can of food he ate at the grocery store. _____ (7th), he likes to watch _____ and was probably at the Picture Plex downtown. _____ (8th), he's probably an animal lover since he wrote in a note that he enjoyed seeing them at the _____. _____ (9th), he might go to the salon to get his _____ cut. And _____ (10th), he might be driving a _____ since the robberies all happened so quickly.

Thank you, sir. I know I can solve this mystery.

Sincerely,

(Your Name)
Spelling Sleuth

74


www.summerbridgeactivities.com

© RBP Books

## Spelling Sleuth

You did it! The thief was on Long Island. You followed clues to the airport, where you walked up to someone in a tan hat, glasses, and a trench coat. He had letters and words spilling out of his pockets and looked very suspicious. You nabbed him! Let's see what he's got to say about the robberies.

Deer Spelling Sleuth,

I new a smart officer like you wood find the solution! I hope you didn't run out of ink writing down all of the clues! You must have looked north and south while running around on this goose chase, but you found me! I think your teacher would be very proud, two!

Sincerely,

Pal the Printing Pooch

Deer Spelling Sleuth

The thief needed most of the letters and words he borrowed to write this note since dogs don't spell very well!

You should be proud of all of the super sleuth work you've done! Now there is one last challenge. Can you circle the homophones in this letter and spell them correctly below?

_____          _____

_____          _____

# Answer Pages

## Page 3
bed, hat, rug, duck, kid, net, pig, log, mop, ant, Riddle answer: barking lot

## Page 4
Answers will vary.

## Page 5

```
p f r a h s l e m y
k l f d q s v x k e
d l r n o e t b u s
r c i e l m x v i i
o e e s v f e o l i
e n g c j o n o g
j t d y t h e n d u
e h p d r w o m l r
n o e k k e d n e q
k a n y r e v e l i
```

## Page 6
**1.** win    **2.** big    **3.** listen
**4.** grin   **5.** into   **6.** will
**7.** finish **8.** him    **9.** mitt
**10.** list

## Page 7
Answers will vary.

## Page 8
**1.** lunch  **2.** stung  **3.** bug
**4.** nut    **5.** fun    **6.** hungry

## Page 9
sea, whale, tail, bite, eel, float, toad, alive, bored

## Page 10
**1.** rain   **2.** make   **3.** game
**4.** day    **5.** bake   **6.** maybe
**7.** paint  **8.** clay   **9.** say
**10.** name

## Page 11
Answers will vary.

## Page 12
**1.** kite   **2.** dime   **3.** prize   **4.** ride
**5.** wise   **6.** invite **7.** slide   **8.** twice
**9.** hide   **10.** kind

## Page 13
**1.** so     **2.** sold   **3.** door   **4.** row
**5.** floor  **6.** open   **7.** load   **8.** more
**9.** store  **10.** close

## Page 14
**1.** ruler, school   **2.** noon
**3.** use, pool       **4.** Glue
**5.** tune            **6.** too
**7.** tool            **8.** rules

## Page 15
**1.** e, hate   **2.** e, hope   **3.** e, made
**4.** e, ate    **5.** e, cute   **6.** e, dime
**7.** Answer will vary.

## Page 16
Begin sh sound:
ship, shut, she, should
Begin ch sound:
child, chin
Ends sh sound:
fish, wash
Ends ch sound:
much, such, each, beach

## Page 17
**1–5.** Answers will vary.
**6.** while   **7.** which   **8.** whole
**9.** whom    **10.** whose

## Page 18

## Page 19
**1.** cut    **2.** bark   **3.** camp   **4.** rock
**5.** think  **6.** duck   **7.** hike   **8.** pick
**9.** like   **10.** come

# Answer Pages

**Page 20**
1. trash    2. brother    3. train
4. breeze    5. tree

**Page 21**
1. glass    2. planet    3. slow
1. clock    2. close    3. please
1. flew    2. glove    3. slam
1. blast    2. plane    3. slow

**Page 22**
1. swing    2. sport    3. smile
4. slide    5. snow    6. sled

**Page 23**
1. Spr    2. str    3. thr    4. str
5. spr    6. str    7. str    8. thr
9. spr    10. str

**Page 24**
1. knock, Knee    2. know
3. wrap    4. wrist
5. knife    6. write
7. knot    8. wrong

**Page 25**
1. refill    2. unsure    3. unsafe
4. retell    5. redo
6–10. unsaid, uneven, undo, rename,
    reset. Order of answers will vary.

**Page 26**
**Across:** 1. mice 3. circle 5. nice
**Down:** 2. circus 4. cent 6. city

**Page 27**
1. germ    2. large    3. judge
4. gentle    5. age    6. change
7. bridge    8. cage    9. huge
10. giant

**Page 28**
**Column 1**
soon, spoon, room, food, tooth, broom
**Column 2**
look, good, cook, book

**Page 29**
1. cold    2. low    3. old    4. soap
5. coat    6. boat    7. float    8. road
9. toad    10. row    11. hold

**Puzzle**
That was cool!

**Page 30**
about, cloud, outside, town, loud,
sound, crowd, around, now, house, out

**Page 31**
1. draw    2. saw    3. lawn
4. water    5. fall    6. small
7. taught    8. cause    9. all
10. talk    11. walk

**Page 32**
goose, balloon, moose, raccoon, rabbit,
parrot, gorilla, deer, rooster

**Page 33**

```
p q v l g f d q y e
x v t j i s i t m u
d r p a l p n q l h
l j d e i n c g i d
f s i e x l r m a y
m g t s l h l t n s
h c r a i s e w s a
u z p x y k w i z x
g p z s o k t g e r
p y a l p l y u d l
```

1. faint    2. pay    3. weigh

**Page 34**
1. lead    2. year    3. seed    4. deer
5. reach    6. fear    7. ear    8. clear
9. bee    10. near

**Page 35**
Answers will vary.

**Page 36**
1. learn    2. heard    3. shirt
4. girl    5. her    6. worm, dirt
7. turn    8. burn    9. fern
10. work

Spelling Grade 2—RBP3446

# Answer Pages

**Page 37**
Answers will vary.

**Page 38**
1. foot          2. would          3. put
4. could         5. push           6. stood
7. took          8. brook          9. hook
10. full         11. pull

**Page 39**
1. annoy         2. coin           3. toy
4. boy           5. voice          6. join
7. spoil         8. enjoy          9. noise or joy

**Page 40**
Answers order will vary.
1. ju(mp)        2. sto(mp)        3. thu(mp)
4. bu(mp)        5. ra(mp)         6. la(mp)
7. sta(nd)       8. ha(nd)         9. ba(nd)
10. arou(nd)

**Page 41**
1. hint          2. different      3. bank
4. ink           5. shrink         6. sink
7. sank          8. think          9. point
10. drink

**Page 42**
belt, calm, help, elf, felt, quilt, gulp, halt, shelf, myself

**Page 43**
Last, forest, skunk, past, fast, gasp, stump, step, ask  Answer will vary.

**Page 44**
1. doctor        2. dollar         3. teacher
4. singer        5. farmer         6. lawyer
7. sailor        8. dancer         9. actor
10. officer      11. Answer will vary.

**Page 45**
**Long *i* sound:**
sky, fly, by, my, dry
**Long *e* sound:**
candy, happy, hardly, healthy, many, penny

**Page 46**
ball, add, yell, hill, toss, miss, grass, call, pass, well, off, mitt

**Page 47**
1. wish(es)      2. box(es)        3. frog(s)
4. match(es)     5. bug(s)         6. crash(es)

**Page 48**
1. hopped        2. swinging
3. running       4. waved
5. played        6. smiling

**Page 49**
bigger, funnier, messiest, quicker, nicest, widest

**Page 50**
1. hair          2. pair           3. dare
4. chair         5. share          6. scare
7. stare         8. stairs         9. air
10. care

**Page 51**
1. le, able      2. le, wiggle
3. le, bubble    4. le, puzzle
5. le, table     6. le, rattle
7. le, trouble   8. le, tickle
9. le, bottle    10. le, little

**Page 52**
1. flies         2. skies          3. carries
4. tried         5. cried          6. cherries
7. babies        8. ladies         9. pies
10. fried

**Page 53**
1. lives         2. leaves         3. shelves
4. calves        5. wives          6. halves

**Page 54**
1. ph    2. ph    3. ph    4. gh
5. gh    6. ph    7. gh    8. gh
9. gh    10. gh

# Answer Pages

## Page 55
1. shoe    2. new    3. chew
4. drew    5. few

## Page 56
1. piece    2. mail    3. sea    4. son
5. red    6. buy    7. there

## Page 57
1. I'm    2. It's    3. She'll
4. You're    5. Don't    6. We're
7. can't    8. I'll    9. He'd
10. isn't

## Page 58
1. cupcake    2. thing
3. one    4. weekend
5. birth    6. friend
7. inside    8. my

## Page 59
1. mat    2. pen    3. wealthy
4. mouse    5. long  Answers will vary.

## Page 60
1. Allie    2. third    3. sixth
4. Lori    5. fourth    6. second
7. fifth    8. first

## Page 61
1. Thursday    2. Saturday
3. Tuesday    4. Friday
5. Monday    6. Wednesday
7. week
8. Answer will vary.

## Page 62
The man in a trench coat wearing a hat because the letter was signed Mr. X.

## Page 63
red, black, tan, etc.

## Page 64
1. corn
2. pears
3. pickles
4. string beans
5. peaches
6. cherries
7. squash
8. crushed pineapple
9. spiced pumpkin

## Page 65
Car B—Drive north to exit 3.
Car C—Drive north to exit 2.
Car D—Drive south to exit 4.
Car E—Drive north to exit 1.
Words with th: then, the, with, through, that, thin, than, path, north, south, etc.

## Page 66
when, why, where, who, whom, what, which, whose, etc.

## Page 67
teacher, officer, lawyer, farmer, sailor, banker, doctor, singer. All the words have the "er" sound.

## Page 68
moose, sheep, parrot, raccoon, rabbit, rooster, gorilla, butterfly, goose, deer. All the animal names have double letters in them.

## Page 69
"Meet me at the Laughing Trough Restaurant to talk about the money I want for returning the dog.

A coughing voice on the phone will give you enough information to graph directions to the restaurant. When you meet me there I will be carrying a photo of the missing dog. Signed, Ex"

Bonus: It was signed "Ex," and the thief always signs "X".

# Answer Pages

## Page 70

The hairdresser needs to group the bottles with the same shape together.

## Page 71
2. words like: <u>laugh</u>, gr<u>aph</u>
3. words like: h<u>air</u>, wh<u>ere</u>, t<u>ear</u>
4. words like: c<u>oi</u>l, b<u>oy</u>
5. words like: p<u>u</u>t, c<u>ou</u>ld
6. words like: n<u>ow</u>, b<u>ough</u>
7. words like: g<u>ir</u>l, h<u>ur</u>t, f<u>er</u>n, w<u>or</u>k
8. words like: d<u>eer</u>, f<u>ear</u>
9. words like: pl<u>ay</u>, r<u>ai</u>n
10. words like: l<u>aw</u>n, c<u>au</u>se

## Page 72
"Com<u>e</u> s<u>ee</u> the wh<u>a</u>les from the s<u>ea</u> d<u>i</u>ve and fl<u>oat</u> in our h<u>uge</u> pool." All the missing letters are long vowel sounds. The word thief went to Long Island.

## Page 73
Clues: <u>board</u>walk, <u>camp</u>ground, fair-<u>grounds</u>, side<u>walk</u>, flower <u>bed</u>, <u>super</u>-market, down<u>town</u>, free<u>way</u>, <u>fire</u>house, <u>air</u>port

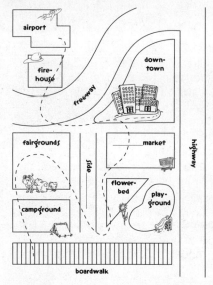

## Page 74
First, dog. Second, man. Third, hat. Fourth, letters. Fifth, Long. Sixth, stew. Seventh, movies. Eighth, zoo. Ninth, hair. Tenth, car.

## Page 75
Deer, Dear
new, knew
wood, would
two, too